World in Focus
Pakistan

SALLY MORGAN

WAYLAND

First published in 2007 by Wayland, an imprint of Hachette Children's Books

Hachette Children's Books, 338 Euston Road, London NW1 3BH

Wayland Australia, Hachette Children's Books, Level 17/207 Kent Street, Sydney, NSW 2000

Commissioning editor: Nicola Edwards
Editor: Nicola Barber
Inside design: Chris Halls, www.mindseyedesign.co.uk
Cover design: Hodder Wayland
Series concept and project management by EASI-Educational Resourcing
(info@easi-er.co.uk)
Statistical research: Anna Bowden
Maps and graphs: Martin Darlison, Encompass Graphics

Printed and bound in China

British Library Cataloguing in Publication Data
Morgan, Sally
  Pakistan. - (World in focus)
  1.Pakistan - Juvenile literature
  I.Title
  954.9'1053

ISBN-13: 978-0-7502-4743-6

Printed and bound in China

Cover top: A worker in a cotton field near Multan picks the delicate cotton off the plants by hand.
Cover bottom and title page: The Badshahi Mosque in Lahore, built by the Mughals in 1674, is still the largest mosque in Pakistan.

The author and publisher would like to thank the following for allowing their pictures to be reproduced in this publication:
Corbis *title page*, 10 (Olivier Matthys/epa), 4, 14 (Galen Rowell), 5 (Lynsey Addario), 6 (Ali Imam/Reuters), 8 (Diego Lezama Orezzoli), 9 (Burstein Collection), 11, 12, 13 (Bettmann), 15, 18, 19 (Ed Kashi), 16, 42 (Mohsin Raza/Reuters), 17 (Amiruddim Mughal/Reuters), 20 (Jonathan Blair), 21, 33, 41, 47 (Akhtar Soomro/epa), 22, 35, 37 (Reuters), 23 (HO/Reuters), 24, 44 (Arshad Arbab/epa), 25, 34, 46, 58 (Mian Khursheed/Reuters), 26, 27 (Rizwan Saeed/Reuters), 28 (Christine Osborne), 29, 39, 55, 57 (Jonathan Blair), 30 (Asim Tanveer/Reuters), 31 (Rahat Dar/epa), 32 (Mimi Mollica), 36, 49 (Zahid Hussein/Reuters), 38 (Athar Hussain/X01601/Reuters), 40 (David Cumming/Eye Ubiquitous), 43 (epa), 45 (Tom Pietrasik), 48, 56 (Maher Attar/MGA Production), 50 (Munish Sharma/Reuters), 51 (Matthieu Paley), 52 (Olivier Matthys/epa), 53 (Paul Almasy), 54 (Shabbir Hussain Imam/epa), 59 (Shawn Thew/epa).

The directional arrow portrayed on the map on page 7 provides only an approximation of north.

The data used to produce the graphics and data panels in this title werethe latest available at the time of production.

CONTENTS

CHAPTER 1

Pakistan – An Overview

Pakistan is the seventh largest country in Asia and occupies a position of great strategic importance. It lies between the Himalaya Mountains and the Arabian Sea and is bordered by Iran to the west, Afghanistan to the northwest, China to the northeast and India to the east.

The River Indus runs though the centre of Pakistan and some time around 4000 BC, people settled in its valley and developed one of the earliest civilizations in the world (see page 8). The people of the Indus Valley civilization farmed the rich soils of the river plains and used the river as a trade route to the sea. Since then the plains of the Indus have been fought over and conquered by many different people including Arabs, Mughals and the British.

Each of these conquering peoples has left their own distinctive mark on the culture of the region. Today, the population of Pakistan is made up of many different groups, each of which has its own culture and language.

YEARS OF STRUGGLE

From the mid-19th century, the region was part of British India. The modern country of Pakistan was created in 1947 when British India was divided into two separate countries – India and Pakistan. Pakistan was originally made up of two parts. One part was West Pakistan which extended from the Himalayas along the Indus Valley to the coast. The other, East Pakistan, was a completely separate area between India and Myanmar (Burma). The name 'Pakistan' was created using letters taken

► Two men cross a wooden footbridge over the Indus River in Baltistan, in the Northern Areas of Pakistan. The Indus flows from the mountains southwards to the coast near Karachi.

from the names of the different states of the country, namely Punjab, Afghania (North West Frontier Province), Kashmir, Sindh, and Baluchistan. The letter 'i' was added later to make the word easier to pronounce. In Urdu, the national language of the country, the words *pak* and *stan* mean 'pure' and 'country'.

The years since independence have been eventful. There have been continual political struggles; democratically elected governments have been ousted by the military, politicians have been accused of corruption and there have been assassination attempts on a president. There have been internal struggles as East Pakistan broke away to form Bangladesh (see page 12) and as some groups demanded greater representation and even independence.

▲ A truck carrying passengers in Karachi. All forms of transport are seen in Pakistan's cities.

There have been wars, too. Within a year or so of independence Pakistan was at war with its close neighbour, India, over the mountainous region of Kashmir (see page 13). Ever since then Kashmir has been partly occupied by both countries and there have been numerous border disputes, the most serious during the 1990s. Despite years of talks, the problem has still not been resolved.

Pakistan has had close links with Afghanistan for hundreds of years and, not surprisingly, it has been caught up in the struggles taking place in that country. Not least, it has had to cope with the millions of refugees that have fled across the border to the safety of Pakistan (see page 19).

GLOBAL SIGNIFICANCE

Pakistan is overwhelmingly Muslim and only a small percentage of people follow other religions, such as Christianity or Hinduism. Pakistan has the second largest Muslim population in the world (after Indonesia) and, as such, the country has an important voice in the Islamic world.

For a long time the world powers were not really interested in Pakistan as it was a poor, agricultural nation. But that has changed. Modern-day Pakistan has a booming economy and it occupies an important strategic position between the Middle East and India. Pakistan now has the attention of China and the United States, both countries that are trying to increase their influence in South Asia.

PROBLEMS AHEAD

With nearly 166 million people living in an area slightly less than double the size of California, Pakistan is not without its problems. Birth and death rates are high and nearly 40 per cent of the population is under the age of 15. Many millions of people live in poverty. The towns and cities are getting larger but there is little in the way of urban planning. Streets are congested with traffic, and water supplies and sewage systems are often inadequate. Industrial development is taking place at an incredible rate but there are few environmental controls. As a result there is widespread disease and pollution.

Physical geography

- Land area: 778,720 sq km/ 300,664 sq miles
- Water area: 25,220 sq km/ 9,737 sq miles
- Total area: 803,940 sq km/ 310,402 sq miles
- World rank (by area): 35
- Land boundaries: 6,774 km/ 4,209 miles
- Border countries: Afghanistan, China, India, Iran
- Coastline: 1,046 km/ 650 miles
- Highest point: K2 (8,611 m/ 28,251 ft)
- Lowest point: Indian Ocean (0 m/ 0 ft)

Source: CIA World Factbook

▶ Muslims pray at Friday prayers in Peshawar. Islam plays an important role in the daily lives of the people of Pakistan.

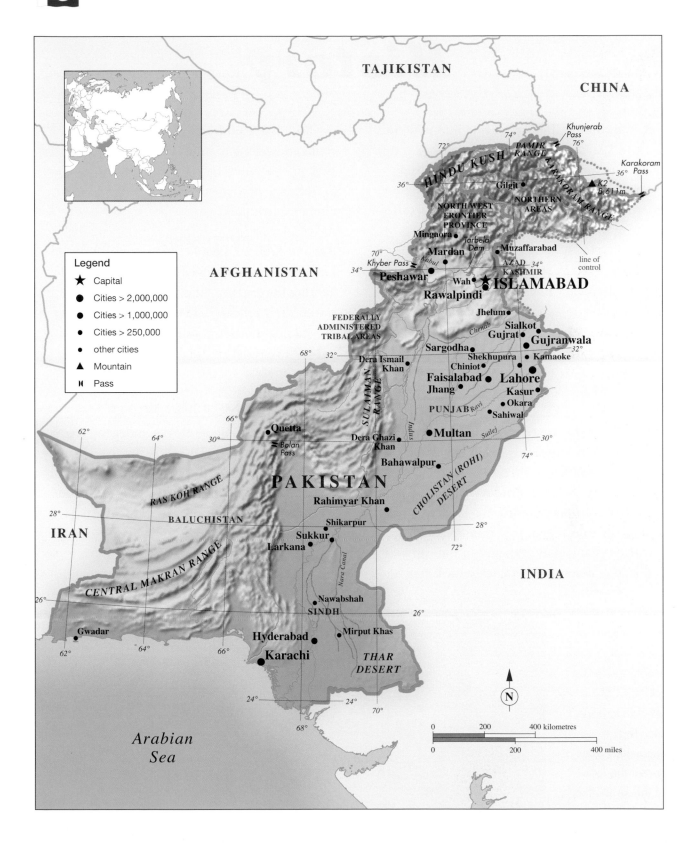

TAJIKISTAN

CHINA

Khunjerab
Pass
76°

PAMIR
RANGE

HINDU KUSH

72°

74°

Karakoram
Pass

36°

36°

K2
8,611m

Gilgit

KARAKORAM RANGE

NORTHERN
AREAS

NORTH WEST
FRONTIER
PROVINCE

Mingaora

70°

Tarbela
Dam

Muzaffarabad

AFGHANISTAN

Mardan

line of
control

Khyber Pass

Kabul

34°

AZAD
KASHMIR

34°

Peshawar

Wah

ISLAMABAD

Rawalpindi

Jhelum

Chenab

Sialkot

FEDERALLY
ADMINISTERED
TRIBAL AREAS

68°

32°

Sargodha

Gujrat

Gujranwala

32°

Dera Ismail
Khan

Shekhupura

Kamaoke

Chiniot

SULAIMAN RANGE

Faisalabad

Lahore

Jhang

Kasur

PUNJAB

Okara

Ravi

Sahiwal

Legend

★ Capital

● Cities > 2,000,000

● Cities > 1,000,000

• Cities > 250,000

· other cities

▲ Mountain

Ɪ Pass

Quetta

66°

Bolan
Pass

30°

Dera Ghazi
Khan

Multan

Sutlej

30°

74°

Bahawalpur

PAKISTAN

RAS KOH RANGE

Rahimyar Khan

CHOLISTAN (ROHI) DESERT

Indus

28°

BALUCHISTAN

Shikarpur

28°

72°

IRAN

CENTRAL MAKRAN RANGE

Sukkur

Larkana

64°

62°

66°

INDIA

Nara Canal

26°

Nawabshah

26°

Gwadar

SINDH

62°

64°

66°

Mirput Khas

Hyderabad

THAR
DESERT

Karachi

24°

24°

70°

N

68°

Arabian
Sea

0   200   400 kilometres

0   200   400 miles

CHAPTER 2

History

As a country, Pakistan came into existence in 1947, but the history of the region that makes up modern-day Pakistan dates back thousands of years, and it includes numerous invasions, military overthrows and times of political instability.

EARLY HISTORY

The Indus Valley has an important role in the history of the region. It extends from the Himalayas in the north to the coast, and it was the site of two of the earliest settlements, Harappa and Moenjodaro, which date back to between 4000 and 2000 BC. The first settlers were farmers, attracted by the rich soils that had been built up by the river. Soon more people moved into the area and settlements formed along the river. Over time, the settlements grew into large, well-planned cities with paved main streets, watchtowers, houses and meeting halls. This civilization extended from the valley, towards what is now Iran and into northwest India. The cities traded by sea with Egypt and the Middle East. However, the Indus Valley civilization came to a sudden end around 1700 BC, possibly as a result of devastating floods or a change in the course of the River Indus after an earthquake.

Around 1700 BC, people from central Asia known as Aryans moved into the Indus Valley looking for grazing land for their herds of cattle. They followed a religion in which they prayed to a mother goddess, which is believed to be the foundation for Hinduism. By 900 BC, the Aryans had spread across northern India.

GREAT CONQUERORS

The Macedonian general Alexander the Great (356-323 BC) was a great conqueror who led his army across the Middle East and Asia, creating a huge empire. In 327 BC he entered the Indus Valley where he defeated the army of King Porus, who ruled the region. King Porus used 200 war elephants in the battle which so terrified Alexander's exhausted troops that,

► The ruins of the city of Moenjodaro are a UNESCO World Heritage site. The excavated ruins reveal the layout of the sprawling site, with its network of narrow streets.

despite their victory, they mutinied and refused to go any further. By this time Alexander's empire stretched from Central Europe, south to Egypt and east to the Punjab, all linked together by a network of trade routes. But after Alexander's death, his empire was torn apart in the power struggles of his successors.

In the Indus Valley, power passed to Chandragupta Maurya in 322 BC, when he overthrew the royal family of Magadha that had ruled an Indian kingdom to the east since 700 BC. Chandragupta founded the Mauryan Empire. In 272 BC the Mauryan emperor Ashoka came to power. He was an astute warrior, and expanded his empire in a series of campaigns. But after witnessing the carnage that resulted from the last of his conquests, he converted to the new religion of Buddhism and changed his ways. He helped the spread of Buddhism through South Asia by following Buddhist teachings and by building Buddhist monasteries and *stupas* (memorial buildings).

MANY INVASIONS

Over the next few hundred years the region experienced many invasions, mostly by armies from Europe and Central Asia. Towns and cities were frequently ransacked and people

▲ This sculpture of the Buddha's head dates from the second or third century AD and comes from northern Pakistan.

killed. The conquerors brought with them their own languages, cultures and religions. The invading armies included the Greeks in 195 BC, the Scythians from Central Asia in 75 BC, and in 50 BC, the powerful Parthians from east of the Caspian Sea. In AD 120 the Parthians were themselves defeated by the Kushans, a people from China. The Kushans established an empire that covered present-day Afghanistan, Pakistan and northwest India, and under their rule trade flourished, in particular with the Romans. In the 5th century AD White Huns, horse-riding nomads from Central Asia, invaded from the north. They, in turn, were defeated by the Sassanians from Persia, and by Turks from the eastern Mediterranean. Finally the region was divided into small kingdoms, each with a Hindu ruler.

UNDER MUSLIM RULE

During the 7th century, Arab armies marched across the Middle East into Persia (now Iran), Afghanistan and India. The Arabs followed the new religion of Islam which had started in the Arabian peninsula in the 600s. By 724, the Indus Valley was under the control of a Muslim Arab governor. For about 300 years, the region was divided into two parts. The northern region of Punjab remained under Hindu control, while the south (Multan, Sindh and Baluchistan) was under Muslim rule. However, the ruler of the state of Ghazni (in present-day Afghanistan), Mahmud Ghaznavi, invaded the Hindu territories of the Punjab and Kashmir and then took control of Baluchistan, creating a state which ruled this region until 1187.

THE SULTANATE PERIOD

The armies of Muhammad of Ghor, invading from Afghanistan, ended the rule of the Ghaznavid Empire. Muhammad's successors established the Delhi Sultanate (1206-1526) in which the region was divided up into states, and each state was headed by a sultan (a Muslim head of state). The sultan was responsible for the protection of the state and of Islam, for enforcing laws and collecting taxes.

THE MUGHAL EMPIRE

In 1526 the Mughal Empire was founded when the last of the sultans was defeated by Babur, a Muslim ruler from Central Asia whose ancestors included the Mongol emperors Genghis Khan and Timur. Babur conquered the Punjab and much of northern India, and the expansion of the Mughal Empire continued under his successors, notably Akbar (ruled 1556-1605). By 1707 the Mughal Empire stretched across Afghanistan, Punjab, Sindh and Baluchistan, as well as much of India. Under Mughal rule, architecture flourished and some stunning buildings were constructed, including many in Lahore. However, from the beginning of the 18th century the power of the Mughal rulers began to diminish.

BRITISH RULE

Around 1600, the British established a trading partnership with the Mughals. Over the years, the level of trade increased greatly and the British gradually became involved in the politics of the region. As the Mughals started to lose power, there was instability in the region and the British took advantage of this, gradually taking control of large areas. In 1857,

▼ One of the many buildings built by the Mughals was the Badshahi Mosque in Lahore, completed in 1674. This beautiful mosque is still the largest in Pakistan.

the War of Independence broke out when there was an uprising by both Indian soldiers and local people against the British. It ended in 1858, when the British captured and killed the local rulers who they believed were behind the uprising, but not before many thousands of people were killed, including women and children. After this, the British claimed sovereignty over much of what is now India and Pakistan, then known as British India.

HINDUS AND MUSLIMS

Although British India was under British rule, from 1909 Indians were given limited roles in central and provincial governments. Many Indian Muslims wanted to play a part in government and still retain their religious identity. The Indian National Congress, founded in 1885, was dominated by Hindus, so

in 1907 the All-India Muslim League was established. Initially, the main aim of the League was to co-operate with the Hindus to gain independence for India from British rule. However, religious and cultural differences, and the fact that Hindus far outnumbered Muslims, led many Muslims to believe that it would be impossible to have equality with Hindus in India. So the Muslims started to campaign for a new Muslim state that would combine North West Frontier Province, Baluchistan, Punjab and Sindh, and Bengal (on the east side of India). During the 1940s, Mohammed Ali Jinnah emerged as the leader of the Muslims. He threatened a civil war in India if the British did not give Pakistan its independence. Finally, in 1947, the British government agreed to divide India into separate parts, a process known as Partition. The result

Focus on: The Problems of Partition

In 1947, when British India was divided into the two independent nations of Pakistan and India, there were millions of Muslims and Hindus living on the 'wrong' side of the new borders. As a result, about 3.5 million Hindus and Sikhs fled across the border to India, while 5 million Muslims moved to the new Islamic nation of Pakistan. During this mass migration, violence between Hindus and Muslims left more than half a million people dead.

▶ Indian refugees crowd on to trains at Amritsar, India, in October 1947. During Partition, millions of Muslims and Hindus fled across the new border.

was the secular nation of India and the smaller Muslim nation of Pakistan. Pakistan was made up of East and West Pakistan (see page 4). Mohammed Ali Jinnah became the country's governor-general. Pakistan's first constitution was published in 1956, when the country officially became the Islamic Republic of Pakistan.

EAST PAKISTAN

The physical separation of about 1,600 km (1,000 miles) between East and West Pakistan, and differences in language, culture and wealth between the two regions, caused major political, economic and social conflicts within Pakistan. In elections in 1970, the Awami League won nearly all of the seats in East Pakistan, giving it a majority in the Pakistani government despite having no representatives in West Pakistan. When the West Pakistanis refused to hand over power to Sheikh Mujib, the leader of the Awami League, there was unrest in East Pakistan. The Pakistan army, which was mostly made up of West Pakistanis, moved into East

Pakistan to put down the uprising, and Sheikh Mujib and other Awami League leaders were arrested. In March 1971, East Pakistan declared its independence and war followed. The Indian army invaded in December 1971 and quickly defeated the West Pakistani forces. As a result, East Pakistan officially became the independent country of Bangladesh on 16 December 1971. At the same time West Pakistan became known as Pakistan.

MARTIAL LAW

On several occasions, the military has taken power and governed Pakistan. The first time was in 1958 when government corruption had become widespread, after which there were four years of martial law (government by the military). Political disputes forced the military to take over again in 1969. But after the embarrassing defeat in East Pakistan, the

▼ People in Dhaka cheer some of the men who helped East Pakistan gain its independence in December 1971.

military government stepped down and, in 1971, Zulfiqar Ali Bhutto became president. In 1977, Bhutto was overthrown in a coup led by General Zia-ul-Haq who imposed martial law. General Zia started a programme of Islamization in which Islam played a greater role in everyday life, for example the teaching of Islamic Studies and Arabic became compulsory. Women, who already had fewer rights than men, found that their freedom was greatly curtailed. In 1988, General Zia was killed in a plane crash and Benazir Bhutto, daughter of Zulfiqar Ali Bhutto, became the first woman to govern an Islamic country. She finally lost power in 1996 on charges that her government was corrupt and mismanaged.

General Pervez Musharraf seized power in 1999 (see box). Since the terrorist attacks of 11 September 2001 in the United States, Musharraf has been a strong supporter of the United States in its so-called 'war on terrorism'. In 2004, Shaukat Aziz became prime minister and declared his aim to provide good government, legal and police systems and opportunities for the people of Pakistan.

▲ In September 1988, Benazir Bhutto was elected prime minister of Pakistan. At the time she was one of the most high-profile women leaders in the world.

Focus on: Problems in Kashmir

At the time of Partition there were disputes over several states, one of which was Kashmir. Kashmir had a Hindu ruler, but the majority of its people were Muslim and there were more ties with Pakistan than with India, both geographically and economically. While many people in Kashmir hoped for independence from both countries, Kashmir's ruler decided to sign over the state to India. Pakistan refused to accept the decision and in 1948 war broke out. Kashmir has remained partly occupied by the two countries ever since. The part occupied by Pakistan is called Azad (Free) Kashmir. There was a second war between the two countries in 1965, and there have been many border disputes, the most serious of which occurred in the late 1990s when India and Pakistan moved thousands of troops into the region. Prime Minister Nawaz Sharif negotiated with India over Kashmir, but Pakistan's military did not like the terms to which he agreed resulting, in 1999, in the coup led by General Pervez Musharraf.

CHAPTER 3

Landscape and Climate

Pakistan is a land of contrasts. Mountains dominate its northern regions, while the Thar Desert lies to the east and the mighty Indus River flows through the middle of the country.

MOUNTAINOUS NORTH

The northern highlands of Pakistan include parts of the Hindu Kush, the Karakoram and Pamir ranges, and the Himalayas. These mountain ranges contain 13 of the world's highest peaks, including K2 at 8,611 m (28,251 ft), which is the second highest mountain in the world after Mount Everest, and the highest in Pakistan. In the Himalayas, Nanga Parbat rises to 8,126 m (26,660 ft), while at 7,708 m (25,228 ft)

Tirich Mir is the highest mountain in the Hindu Kush. More than half of the peaks in Pakistan exceed 4,500 m (14,764 ft), and more than 50 peaks reach above 6,500 m (21,325 ft).

? Did you know?

Nanga Parbat ('Naked Mountain' in Urdu) in the western Himalayas is nicknamed the 'killer mountain' as it claimed as many as 50 lives before it was first successfully climbed by an Austrian mountaineer, Hermann Buhl, in 1953.

▼ A group of mountaineers and porters cross the lower slopes of K2, in the Karakoram mountains in the far northeast of Pakistan.

◀ Wells are the only source of water in the desert areas of Pakistan. This well lies in the Cholistan (Rohi) Desert in Punjab Province.

These huge mountain ranges create a barrier between Pakistan and India and Central Asia to the north. There are a number of important high routes, called passes, over the mountains. The main pass is the Karakoram Pass (5,575 m/18,290 ft) that links Kashmir to China. The Khunjerab Pass (4,700 m/15,420 ft), is found on the Pakistan to China route. In the northwest, the Khyber Pass (1,072 m/3,517 ft) links Peshawar in Pakistan with Jalalabad in Afghanistan, where it connects to a route leading to the Afghan capital, Kabul. The Bolan Pass (1,792 m/5,879 ft) provides an essential internal link between the two provinces of Baluchistan and Sindh.

ARID REGIONS

The Thar, or Great Indian, Desert stretches between northwestern India and southeastern Pakistan. In Pakistan it extends into the eastern part of Sindh Province and the southeastern portion of Punjab Province. About 10 per cent of the desert is covered in sand dunes, the highest in the south being about 150 m (492 ft) in height. The rest of the desert is mostly stony desert with rock outcrops and salt pans. A belt of thorn scrub forest lies around the desert. Some of the desert is irrigated so that people can farm and keep cattle and sheep. In the southwest of Pakistan, Baluchistan is a sparsely populated and barren region with rugged mountains, some fertile river valleys and desert. It is, however, the location of valuable mineral reserves (see page 26).

THE INDUS VALLEY

The Indus River is the lifeline of Pakistan as the river and its tributaries provide water to two-thirds of the country. The Indus rises in Tibet, and flows through Kashmir into Pakistan. Then it flows south down the entire length of Pakistan, a distance of about 2,900 km (1,802 miles). The river forms a large delta just before it reaches the Arabian Sea. Over centuries, silt dropped by the waters of the river as they flow downstream has formed a large, fertile plain.

▲ Monsoon rains have flooded this street in Lahore, but daily life goes on as normal.

However, the amount of silt deposited by the river has fallen in recent years due to the building of dams upstream. In time, this will reduce the fertility of the soils and farmers may have to use artificial fertilizers. All of Pakistan's major rivers flow into the Indus, including the Kabul, Jhelum, Chenab, Ravi and Sutlej.

CLIMATE

The climate varies hugely across Pakistan. Precipitation ranges from 150 to 200 mm (6 to 7.9 in) per annum in coastal areas to 1,500 mm (59 in) in the mountains, while the winter to summer average temperatures range from -20°C to 0°C (-4°F to 32°F) in the north and from 14°C to 35°C (57°F to 95°F) in the south.

Much of Pakistan, including Punjab Province, lies in the temperate zone where there are three main seasons; cool and mostly dry from October to February, hot and dry between March and June, and wet and hot from July to September. Islamabad, in the Punjab, has a temperature range from an average 9°C (48.2°F) in January to an average high of 32.5°C (90.5°F) in June. The spring monsoon (a period of heavy rainfall) usually starts around May or June and most of the annual rainfall occurs from July to September. The rest of the year has much less rain – about 50 mm (2 in) per month, or less. However, the monsoon is unreliable and some years it fails to arrive altogether, while in others it causes torrential floods.

WATER SHORTAGES

Water supply is a major issue in Pakistan as there is insufficient rainfall to support the level of farming needed to grow the country's food and cotton crops, especially in the arid regions around the Thar Desert and in parts of Sindh and Baluchistan. As a result, Pakistan relies on an extensive irrigation system (see page 29) using river water from the Indus and its tributaries. However, the flow of water in the Indus is highly erratic. It depends on meltwater from the mountains and from the monsoon rains. In some years, the flow of water may be as high as 223 million cubic metres (7.9 billion cubic feet), while in other years it can fall to as little as 116 million cubic metres (4.1 billion cubic feet) and no water flows down the river into the sea for several months of the year.

Did you know?

The word Punjab means the 'land of five waters', after the five rivers that cross the state: the Indus, Jhelum, Chenab, Ravi and Sutlej.

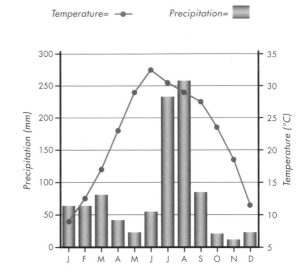

Temperature= ●   Precipitation= ▪

▲ Average monthly climate conditions in Islamabad.

Focus on: The 2005 earthquake

Much of northern Pakistan lies in an earthquake zone, so earthquakes are relatively common. In October 2005, the region along the border with Kashmir was struck by an earthquake measuring 7.6 on the Richter scale, the largest ever to occur in Pakistan. The damage was widespread and at least 73,000 people were killed and up to 100,000 injured in Pakistan and Azad Kashmir. More than 4 million were left homeless. It was estimated in December 2005 that in excess of US$5 billion was needed to repair and rebuild in this already poor region.

▶ A month after the 2005 earthquake, a survivor searches the remains of his house in the Neelum Valley, north of Muzaffarabad in Azad Kashmir, looking for useful items such as clothes and cooking utensils.

CHAPTER 4

Population and Settlements

Pakistan is home to nearly 166 million people and has one of the world's fastest growing populations. The current rate of population growth is just over 2 per cent, compared with just 0.28 per cent in the United Kingdom and 0.92 per cent in the United States. At this rate, the population of Pakistan could double by the year 2035. This rapidly increasing population is putting incredible pressure on the environment and resources, as well as on services such as schools and hospitals.

CULTURAL GROUPS

The population of Pakistan is a mixture of many different groups. The main groups include the Punjabis, Sindhis, Pathans (also called Pashtuns), Mohajirs and Baluchis. Within these five main groups are a number of sub-groups creating a multi-layered cultural mix based on religion, language and ethnic origin.

The Punjabis make up the largest group in Pakistan, with 48 per cent of the population. They live mostly in Punjab Province and they have their own language, Punjabi. However, many Punjabis both read and speak Urdu, the national language of Pakistan while a small percentage are also fluent English-speakers, English being the language most often used for official purposes. Punjabis predominate in Pakistan's military and government. Sindhis and Pathans are the next largest groups, making up 13 per cent and 12.5 per cent of the population respectively. The traditional homeland of the Sindhi people is the province of Sindh in the southeast of Pakistan. Sindhis are

Population data

- Population: 165.8 million
- Population 0-14 yrs: 39%
- Population 15-64 yrs: 57%
- Population 65+ yrs: 4%
- Population growth rate: 2.1%
- Population density: 196.4 per sq km/ 508.7 per sq mile
- Urban population: 34%
- Major cities: Karachi 11,819,000
              Lahore 6,373,000
              Faisalabad 2,533,000

Source: United Nations and World Bank

◄ Crowds of people walk along Anarkali Street, in Lahore in 2004.

mostly rural people with a rich literature and traditions. They prefer to read and write in their own language, Sindhi. The Pathans are found in the mountainous north of Pakistan. There are many Pathan sub-groups, each one with its own language. Pathans are mostly farmers, traders or soldiers in the Pakistani army.

MIGRANTS

Mohajirs (meaning 'refugees' or 'immigrants' in Arabic) are Muslims who migrated from India to the newly formed Pakistan after 1947. They make up about 8 per cent of the population and are concentrated mostly in the cities of Sindh Province, such as Karachi and Hyderabad. They came originally from a variety of different ethnic backgrounds and as a result they have no strong cultural identity, although they all speak Urdu as their native language. So many Mohajirs arrived and settled in Sindh Province in the late 1940s that they outnumbered the native Sindhi people. The Sindhi resented their political and economic influence in the cities and this caused unrest which increased during the 1960s, and continued until very recently. Many Pakistanis still consider the Mohajirs to be 'outsiders'.

However, many Mohajirs have important roles in government, for example Pervez Musharraf (see page 23) comes from a Mohajir family.

▲ Every year, hundreds of tribesmen from Baluchistan, Sindh and Punjab travel with their camels and horses to the Sibi Mela Camel Festival, about 160 km (100 miles) southeast of Quetta.

? Did you know?

Urdu was chosen to be Pakistan's national language after independence, despite the fact that it was spoken by less than 10 per cent of the population.

Focus on: Afghan refugees

The first Afghan refugees started to arrive in Pakistan after the Soviet invasion of Afghanistan in 1979. Over the next 20 years, millions of Afghans fled their country, although many returned after the fall of the Taliban in 2001. Despite a programme of repatriation, 1 million refugees remain in the camps. Each year, it costs millions of dollars to provide shelter, food, health care and other services to the refugees. In 2006 the Pakistani government started another programme of repatriation, with the target of returning 400,000 people.

Baluchis form just 4 per cent of the population of Pakistan. They are a mostly nomadic people, herding livestock on the arid Baluchistan Plateau. Most Baluchis speak Baluchi, a language that is similar to Persian. They are the least educated and poorest sector of the population, with poor representation in government.

EXPANDING CITIES

The urban population of Pakistan is growing rapidly. This is a result of people from rural areas moving to cities for jobs and a consequence of the mass movement of Muslims from India, as many Mohajirs settled in cities in the south. By 2005 about 34 per cent of the Pakistani population lived in cities. The growth rate of the urban population is 4.4 per cent compared with 2.4 per cent in rural areas. However, about 40 per cent of the urban population lives in slums – densely populated areas with makeshift housing and few services.

▼ The flat roofs of these houses in Altit, in the Northern Areas of Pakistan, are used for drying fruits in the sun.

THE CAPITAL CITY

After independence and until 1959, Pakistan's capital city was Karachi in Sindh Province in the far south of the country. In 1959, a decision was made to build a new capital city, Islamabad, to reflect the new Pakistan. Islamabad was built in the northwest of the country at the crossroads between Punjab and the North West Frontier Province. This modern city was built beside the ancient city of Rawalpindi, reflecting the country's past and present. Construction started

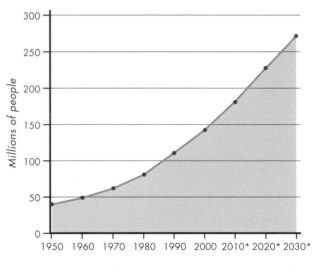

* Projected population

▲ Population growth 1950-2030

Focus on: Karachi – land issues

Karachi is a rapidly expanding city but much of its development is unplanned. A major problem is that too much land is being sold off for development to meet current demands for new housing and industry with little regard for the future. For example, since 2000 about 400 hectares (988 acres) of land that was originally set aside for amenity use such as parks, playgrounds and sport fields has been built on. The infrastructure of the city cannot cope with such rapid expansion. Corruption is another problem, with some developers illegally changing the use of a plot from residential to commercial to make the plot more valuable, and some government officers selling plots of state-owned land at bargain prices as political favours.

► A workman looks out from the shell of a new building overlooking Beach View Park in Karachi in 2005. This is just one of the many tower blocks that are being built in the city.

in 1961 and, in 1967, Islamabad officially became the capital, although work on the city was not completed until the mid-1970s. The city is divided into eight zones, each with its own particular function such as government, commerce, industry or residential.

MAJOR CITIES

Karachi is Pakistan's largest city and main seaport, and is the capital of Sindh Province. It is a major financial, industrial and commercial centre. The other major city in Sindh Province is Hyderabad, which is a manufacturing centre with textile and glass factories. It is also a cultural centre with museums and mosques.

The Punjab lies in the centre of Pakistan and has several large cities, including Lahore,

Pakistan's second largest city and the capital of Punjab Province. Lahore is a cultural and educational centre. It is also the main commercial and banking centre for the province and it serves as a distribution centre for the heavy industry of the surrounding area. Faisalabad is a centre for the textile and fertilizer industries. Multan, in the south of the Punjab, is an ancient city with many Muslim shrines. Rawalpindi in northern Punjab was the temporary capital of Pakistan between 1959 and 1967, while Islamabad was being constructed. It is the headquarters of the Pakistani army and an industrial centre. Peshawar is the capital of the North West Frontier Province. Lying near the Khyber Pass, it is a gateway and important trading centre between Afghanistan and Southeast Asia.

CHAPTER 5

Government and Politics

Pakistan is a federal republic with Islam as its state religion. There has been considerable political turmoil in Pakistan since independence and the country has been ruled by both democratic and military governments. In the ten-year period following independence there were seven different presidents, and this created instability that led to the military taking over.

GOVERNMENT

Pakistan is a federation made up of four self-governing provinces, Baluchistan, Sindh, Punjab and North West Frontier Province; the Federally Administered Tribal Areas (FATA), and Islamabad Capital Territory comprising the capital city. The FATA are located along the border with Afghanistan and are mainly inhabited by Pathan tribes. The Pathans have some degree of independence from central government. Pakistan also has control over Azad Kashmir (see page 13).

The Pakistani parliament is made up of a National Assembly (lower house) and a Senate (upper house). The 342-member National Assembly has 272 members who are directly elected for five years, while the rest are non-elected seats appointed by the political parties. Sixty of these non-elected seats are reserved for women and ten are reserved for non-Muslims. The 100 members of the Senate are chosen by the four Provincial Assemblies, the FATA and the Capital Territory. The Senate members have a six-year term of office.

The president is the head of state, and the prime minister is the chief executive responsible for the day-to-day running of the country. In

▼ The Parliament Buildings in Islamabad. After anti-US violence in 2001, this and other government buildings are guarded by soldiers.

◀ Pakistan's president Pervez Musharraf (left) and prime minister Shaukat Aziz (right) shake hands before Musharraf's visit to the United States in 2005.

2006 the president was Pervez Musharraf and the prime minister was Shaukat Aziz. Under the constitution, the president is elected for a five-year term by the Electoral College of Pakistan, made up of the Senate, the National Assembly and the four Provincial Assemblies. Once elected, the president appoints the leader of the majority party to serve as prime minister. The president is in charge of the country's security and he or she appoints the head of the army, navy and airforce. He or she also has the power to dissolve the National Assembly and call for new elections.

THE CONSTITUTION

Since independence in 1947 Pakistan has had three constitutions which were adopted in 1956, 1962 and 1973 respectively. However, the constitution was suspended in 1977 after a military coup. In 1985, civilian government was re-established and the 1973 constitution was restored, although it was altered to increase the powers of the president. In 1997, the democratically elected members of Parliament amended the constitution to prevent the president from being able to sack the prime minister and dissolve parliament. But within two years there was another military coup and Pervez Musharraf seized power. He suspended the constitution, dissolved the democratically elected parliament and became president. In 2002, Musharraf changed the constitution to strengthen his presidential powers and only then did he allow the constitution to be restored and parliamentary elections to be held.

? Did you know?

In the elections of October 2002, 91 women were elected to be members of the National Assembly, the largest percentage of women in parliament in any Muslim-majority country.

LOCAL GOVERNMENT

Each province has its own Provincial Assembly whose members are elected for five-year terms in local elections. The assemblies are responsible for local matters, such as planning and development, legal systems, and providing schools and hospitals. These services are paid for partly from central government and partly from taxes raised locally. Each assembly elects a chief minister who becomes the executive head of the province. The chief minister nominates a governor.

THE GOVERNMENT AND ISLAM

In some Muslim countries (for example, Saudi Arabia) the laws are based on the Muslim holy book, the Qu'ran. In most Muslim countries, including Pakistan, while the teachings of the Qu'ran make an important contribution to government, the laws of the country are not based entirely on the Qu'ran. However, there is a small minority of radical Muslims in Pakistan who want Pakistan to become a truly Islamic state. For example, in 2003 the Provincial Assembly of North West Frontier Province, where a number of radical Muslims have been elected, voted to introduce Sharia, or Islamic law. This was the first

time this had happened anywhere in Pakistan. Sharia law comes from the teachings of the Qu'ran and is a religious code that governs the way people live, from what they wear to when they pray and how they conduct business. Within Sharia law, certain crimes are punished by specific penalties, for example, theft is punished by cutting off a hand. The cases are heard by a Sharia court. In North West Frontier Province, Sharia law now takes precedence over the existing provincial laws, and every Muslim is bound by it.

MAIN POLITICAL ORGANIZATIONS

There are three main political parties in Pakistan and a number of small parties that are campaigning on specific issues. Currently, the largest party in Parliament is the Pakistan Muslim League (Q) (PML-Q). This party is centre-to-conservative, and it has its origins in the original Muslim League, which was involved in the foundation of Pakistan (see page 11). The PML-Q was formed in 2001, when the Pakistan Muslim League divided into several parties. The PML-Q strongly supports President Pervez

▶ Molana Fazal ur Rehman speaks to supporters during a three-day religious congregation in Peshawar. He is the Secretary General of an Islamic political alliance called Mutahida Majlis-e-Amal.

◀ A Pakistani woman casts her vote during a by-election at a polling station in Sanjawal, Punjab Province, in 2004.

Musharraf, whereas the Pakistan Muslim League (Nawaz) or PML (N), is loyal to Nawaz Sharif. Sharif was twice elected prime minister during the 1990s, but escaped the country when Musharraf overthrew his government.

The Pakistan People's Party (PPP) was formed in 1967 with Zulfiqar Ali Bhutto as its chairman.

It is a socialist party that wants to improve the standard of living of the poor and to give opportunities to all. There are a number of religious parties that want the Muslim religion to have a greater role in everyday life, with Sharia law replacing the existing legal code. Their share of the vote is small, but they have gained power in areas such as North West Frontier Province.

Focus on: Independence movements

There are more than 16 million Pathans living in northern Pakistan and Afghanistan. The Pathans are a fiercely independent people who have a long history of resisting invaders, including the British. In 1902 the British gave the Pathans the region of North West Frontier Province, between the border of British India and Afghanistan. After 1947, a Pathan independence movement, called the Redshirts, was formed to campaign for an independent Pushtunistan. The independence of Bangladesh in 1971 encouraged the Pathans to demand more control over their land, resulting in thousands of armed Pathans clashing with the

Pakistani military, and there has been civil unrest in the region ever since.

There is also a movement for independence in Baluchistan. This is a poor province and its people have seen little benefit from the region's large gas fields. Only 25 per cent of the villages have electricity, and only 20 per cent have safe drinking water. The outlawed Baluchistan Liberation Army carries out frequent attacks on gas pipelines and electricity pylons, often disrupting the flow of oil, gas and electricity to the rest of Pakistan.

CHAPTER 6

Energy and Resources

Pakistan's energy consumption has tripled since 1985 and it is continuing to rise, as industry develops and more villages are connected to the electricity grid. However, Pakistan is not particularly rich in natural resources. It has oil and gas fields, and coal deposits, but oil and coal production is insufficient to meet demand, so Pakistan relies on expensive imports.

FOSSIL FUELS

Pakistan is heavily dependent on imported oil. In 2002 imported oil represented 31 per cent of the country's energy consumption at a cost of US$3,096 billion. The most productive of the country's oil fields is at Dhurnal in Punjab Province, but production is now declining. In contrast, Pakistan's natural gas fields are substantial and at the moment they can supply all the country's needs. However, most of the gas fields are in Baluchistan and pipelines are attacked regularly (see page 25). The gas is distributed via a network of pipelines and is used for electricity generation and industrial uses. Demand for gas is growing at 6.3 per cent per year, and by 2010 Pakistan will have to import gas to make up the shortfall between production and demand.

The largest reserves of coal, about 435 billion tonnes (428 billion tons), are located in Sindh Province, with smaller coal deposits in Punjab

▼ The purification plant at the Sui gas field in Baluchistan in 2006. The average output of this gas field is about 28 million cubic metres (1 billion cubic feet) per day, representing almost 45 per cent of the country's total natural gas production.

◀ Local people wait for news outside a coal mine near Quetta, after an underground gas explosion in 2004. Fifteen miners died in the explosion.

and Baluchistan. However, Pakistani coal is low grade and low value. Most of the coal is used in power stations that generate electricity for the brick-making industry.

MORE ELECTRICITY

In 2004, the Pakistani government published its 25-year Energy Security Plan. There are ambitious plans to increase the electricity generating capacity from 19,000 megawatts to 160,000 megawatts by 2030. The only way this can be achieved without importing more oil is to develop renewable energy sources such as hydroelectric power (HEP), wind and solar energy.

Did you know?

By 2002, less than half of Pakistan's population had access to electricity.

Nuclear power

Nuclear power provides about 2.2 per cent of total electricity production in Pakistan. There are two nuclear power plants, powered by uranium, which is quarried in Pakistan. The first plant, a pressurized water reactor, was built in the 1970s on the coast near Karachi with help from Canadian companies. It has recently been upgraded so it can operate until 2012. The second nuclear plant at Chasma in the Punjab, was built with the help of the Chinese. Pakistan is in negotiations with China to build two more nuclear reactors at the two existing sites. Nuclear power plants generate toxic waste that either has to be placed in underground, long-term storage or sent for reprocessing. The small amount of toxic waste generated by the two nuclear power plants is currently stored.

HEP has the potential to generate up to 50,000 megawatts of electricity, but by 2005 only about 6,500 megawatts were being generated. The two main hydroelectric dams are the Tarbela Dam on the Indus and the Mangla Dam on the Jhelum River in Azad Kashmir. More hydropower schemes are planned, including the Basha Dam, which is upstream from the Tarbela Dam. HEP is a sustainable source of power but there are problems. For example, a dam traps silt in its reservoir rather than the silt being deposited in the river valley, and this gradually reduces the output of the dam. This problem can be addressed by catching the silt before it enters the reservoir, and by planting trees on cleared slopes to stop soil from being eroded. Dams also reduce the flow of water down a river which can interfere with irrigation and disrupt the movement of fish.

RENEWABLE ENERGY

Pakistan aims to generate 5 per cent of electricity using renewable energy sources other than HEP by 2030. For example, two new wind farms under construction in Sindh Province will generate a total of 700 megawatts by 2010. However, about 60 per cent of Pakistan's villages are not connected to the electricity grid and the cost of extending the grid into remote areas is high, so small-scale renewable energy schemes are more appropriate in these areas. For example, micro-wind turbines are being installed in many places in Sindh Province to provide electricity and power for pumping water. Solar power units are being fitted to houses to supply lighting, fans, electric sockets, solar water disinfectant units and solar cookers.

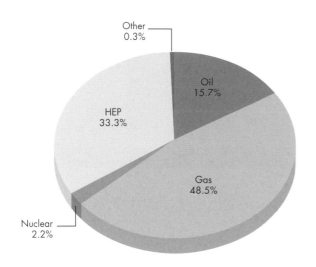

▲ Electricity production by type

Other
0.3%

Oil
15.7%

HEP
33.3%

Gas
48.5%

Nuclear
2.2%

▶ The Tarbela Dam on the Indus River was completed in 1977. It is 148 m (485 ft) high and 2,743 m (9,000 ft) long.

WATER RESOURCES

In 2003 and 2004 there was widespread drought in Sindh Province and the water level in water-bearing rocks (aquifers) fell by 10 m (33 ft). With a population expected to nearly double by 2035, water supplies are critical to Pakistan's survival. As the country's water demands increase, Pakistan needs to start building reservoirs to store large volumes of water. Agriculture uses about 95 per cent of the country's water to irrigate about 14.6 million hectares (36 million acres) of farmland, but the irrigation systems are poorly managed. Up to one-quarter of the irrigated land is waterlogged and this has led to major problems with salinization (see page 55).

▲ In the far north of Pakistan, men dig an irrigation channel to carry water from a glacier to newly planted orchards and fields further down the valley.

Energy data

- ▭ Energy consumption as % of world total: 0.7%
- ▭ Energy consumption by sector (% of total):

Industry:	26.7%
Transportation:	17.3%
Agriculture:	1.4%
Services:	2.5%
Residential:	51.6%
Other:	0.5%

- ▭ CO_2 emissions as % of world total: 0.4%
- ▭ CO_2 emissions per capita in tonnes p.a.: 0.72

Source: World Resources Institute

Focus on: The Indus Waters Treaty

Pakistan depends almost entirely on water from the Indus basin. In 1960, a dispute between Pakistan and India over the use of water from the Indus basin was resolved by the Indus Waters Treaty. Under this treaty, Pakistan receives most of the flow of the Indus, Jhelum and Chenab rivers. However, in 2000 India started construction of the Baglihar Dam on the Jhelum, sparking fears of a 'water war'. In 2005, Pakistan took the issue to the World Bank, which mediated in the original treaty between Pakistan and India. Pakistan claims that the Baglihar Dam will deprive it of water for agriculture and HEP schemes. The Pakistani government also fears that in times of tension, India could use the dam gates to cause a flood or to withhold water. Discussions in 2006 indicated that an agreement was likely.

CHAPTER 7

Economy and Income

In 1947, Pakistan had an agriculture-based economy with virtually no industry and few financial or energy resources. Since then the country's reliance on agriculture has decreased, and industry and manufacturing have steadily developed. In 2005, Pakistan had the second-fastest growing economy in Asia, beaten only by China.

AGRICULTURE

Despite the shift away from agriculture to industry, farming still continues to employ about 50 per cent of the working population.

In 2004, the agricultural contribution to GDP was 22 per cent. The chief crops include cotton, wheat, rice, sugar cane and tobacco. Pakistan is the world's fourth largest cotton producer, and cotton and textiles make up two-thirds of the country's export earnings. The cotton crop covers about 3.2 million hectares (7.9 million acres), most of which is in Punjab Province.

MANUFACTURING AND TRADE

Pakistan's manufacturing capacity has expanded steadily since independence and in 2004-5 it accounted for about 18 per cent

Focus on: Cotton production

In the year 2002 to 2003, Pakistan produced just under 12 million bales of cotton (each bale weighing 170 kg (375 lb)), an increase from about 9.3 million bales in the 1990s. The predicted yield for 2005-6 was estimated to be 15 million bales. This has been achieved by planting more land with higher-yielding cotton varieties, and by improving irrigation and pest control – pests such as the leaf curl virus can destroy thousands of hectares of cotton. The size of the crop is important as it determines the availability and cost of cotton for the country's textile industry, and this in turn influences the value of exports. Despite the increases in yield, the demand for cotton exceeds the domestic harvest, so between 1.2 and 1.5 million bales of high-grade cotton are imported. This makes Pakistan the world's third largest importer of cotton, most of which comes from the United States.

▲ A worker in a cotton field near Multan. The delicate cotton is picked off the plants by hand.

◀ A worker packs boxes with footballs for sale during the 2006 World Cup. About 85 per cent of the world's footballs are manufactured in factories in Sialkot, in Punjab Province.

of GDP. Textiles make up the largest manufacturing sector, followed by cement, sugar and rubber. Manufacturing industries employ just under 20 per cent of the workforce. The main manufacturing centres include Karachi, Hyderabad, and the region around Lahore.

Pakistan has a number of major trading partners, of which Europe, the United States and China are among the largest. The main

imports include wheat, cotton, oil, chemicals, fertilizers, machinery and transport equipment, while exports consist mostly of textile and agricultural products. Pakistan imports a lot of oil (see page 26), mostly from neighbouring Iran. Pakistan has also improved trade with India, for example in 2005 a four-year ban on sugar imports was lifted.

Economic data

- Gross National Income (GNI) in US$: 90,663,000,000
- World rank by GNI: 44
- GNI per capita in US$: 600
- World rank by GNI per capita: 161
- Economic growth: 6.4%

Source: World Bank

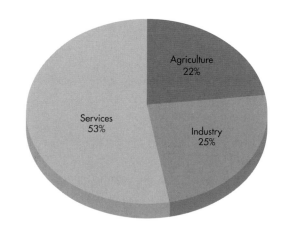

▲ Contribution by sector to national income

Agriculture 22%

Services 53%

Industry 25%

GROWTH RATES

During the 1980s the economy grew at about 6 per cent annually. This high growth rate was created by aid from the United States, money sent back home by Pakistanis working abroad – called remittances – and bumper cotton and wheat crops. During the 1990s the economy slowed, partly as a result of poor management and corruption in the higher levels of government. Since 2000, the growth rate has risen and in 2005 it reached a record high of more than 8 per cent. However, since 2005 inflation has risen to 11 per cent, caused by the increased cost of oil and by food producers limiting the supply of foodstuffs in order to push prices up. Despite the country's record economic growth, unemployment was still at 6.6 per cent in 2005 and there is widespread poverty.

WOMEN AT WORK

Traditionally in Pakistan it is considered improper for a woman to work, although this attitude is changing in some parts of the country, particularly in the cities. Usually, only the poorest women work outside the home, often as midwives, cleaners or nannies. Some women work from home making goods which

Focus on: Pakistanis abroad

During the 1970s there was high unemployment in Pakistan, so the government encouraged workers to travel abroad for work, especially to the Middle East. Today more than 2 million Pakistanis, about 2 per cent of the adult male workforce, live outside Pakistan, three-quarters of them in the Gulf States. Most send back money to their families and for this reason they represent the second largest source of foreign exchange (about US$2.5 billion in 2002). A Pakistani migrant worker usually stays between three and six years in the Middle East and is often then replaced by another family member. Most are unskilled or semi-skilled workers under 30 years of age, often from the northern provinces.

▶ A Pakistani-born bus driver in the UK. Many Pakistanis work abroad.

► A homeless man sleeps next to a busy road in Karachi in 2005. Extreme poverty is a major problem in Pakistan.

they sell to middlemen, often for very little money. Few families admit that their women work for fear of being shamed, and this makes it difficult for poorer women to improve their chances of employment and to be protected against exploitation. However, women from richer families tend to be well-educated, and some have had important roles in government.

DEBT AND POVERTY

Although Pakistan is a growing economy, it has relatively small amounts of money to spend on public services. The army is large and expensive to run, the population is increasing rapidly, and there are millions of Afghan refugees who need both food and shelter (see page 19). The country also has a huge foreign debt, which stood at about US$34 billion in 2005. This means that more than 80 per cent of Pakistan's annual budget is spent on paying back its foreign debt, paying for the army and for general administration, leaving less than 20 per cent for public services such as health and education.

Poverty is a major social problem. In 2002, about 35 per cent of the population – one in every three people – lived below the poverty line of US$2 a day, an increase from 26 per cent in 1988. These people lack sufficient food and access to basic services, schooling and health care. Many of the poor live in rural areas where they are vulnerable to environmental problems such as water pollution and soil erosion (see pages 54-5).

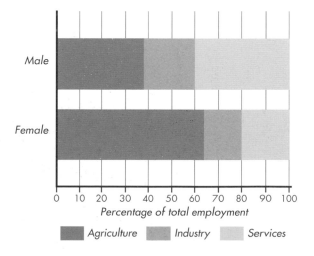

▲ Labour force by sector and gender

CHAPTER 8

Global Connections

Pakistan has a significant voice in the Muslim world and in South Asia, and its control over vital routes through the mountains and access to trade routes through the Arabian Sea make it an important regional power.

INDIA AND PAKISTAN

India and Pakistan have never agreed over the status of Kashmir (see page 13) and there have been border disputes since independence. During the 1990s, diplomatic talks broke down and thousands of troops were moved into the region. Tension grew in 1998 when first India and then Pakistan carried out nuclear tests, resulting in economic sanctions being put in place against both countries by the United States, the European Union and other trading partners. This was the first time that Pakistan had publicly admitted to owning nuclear weapons. In fact, Pakistan had been secretly developing nuclear weapons since the 1970s after India tested its own nuclear device in 1974. In April 1999 when Pakistani soldiers and Kashmiri militants crossed into Indian territory the Indian army attacked, resulting in armed hostilities known as the Kargil Conflict. After a great deal of international diplomacy Pakistan agreed to withdraw in June 1999. But military build-up in the area continued, and by 2002 the two countries had an estimated 1 million troops along the border. However, outright war over Kashmir was averted by ongoing international diplomacy, and in 2004 India and Pakistan agreed to a ceasefire. Since then relations have improved, allowing, for example, cross-border bus services to resume in 2005 (see page 58).

▼ Pakistani soldiers stand at a checkpoint along the Line of Control that divides Pakistani-controlled Kashmir from the Indian-controlled part.

FRIENDS WITH CHINA

After the war with India in 1965 (see page 13), Pakistan developed strong ties with China, and the relationship between the two countries has grown stronger over the years. Today, China is a major trading partner, and it has played a critical role in financing much of Pakistan's industrial development, in particular the building of nuclear reactors (see page 27) and the modernization of the railway network. China benefits through access to important trade routes and greater influence in the region.

AFGHANISTAN

Pathans live in both Afghanistan and Pakistan, so historically there have always been close links between the two countries. When the Soviet Union invaded Afghanistan in 1979 the

▶ Refugees wait to enter Pakistan from Afghanistan at a border crossing in Baluchistan in 2001. Since 1979, more than 3 million Afghan refugees have fled to Pakistan.

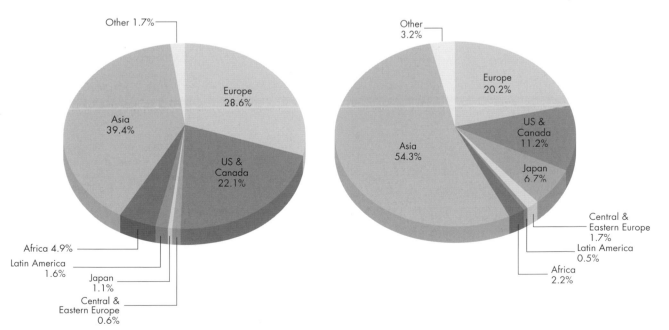

Other 1.7%
Europe 28.6%
Asia 39.4%
US & Canada 22.1%
Africa 4.9%
Latin America 1.6%
Japan 1.1%
Central & Eastern Europe 0.6%

▲ Destination of exports by major trading region

Other 3.2%
Europe 20.2%
US & Canada 11.2%
Japan 6.7%
Asia 54.3%
Central & Eastern Europe 1.7%
Latin America 0.5%
Africa 2.2%

▲ Origin of imports by major trading region

? **Did you know?**

Between 1979 and 1990 more than 3.3 million
Afghan refugees crossed the border into Pakistan.

Pakistani government played a vital role in
supporting anti-Soviet forces and sheltering
millions of Afghan refugees. The Soviet army
withdrew in 1989, but fighting between rival
groups meant that millions of Afghan refugees
remained in Pakistan. In 1996 the Taliban (an
Islamic fundamentalist group) took control and
set up an Islamic government in Afghanistan,
which was supported by Pakistan.

FRIEND OF THE UNITED STATES

The United States has played an important role
in Pakistan since 1947. During the early 1950s
Pakistan was described as the United States'
'most allied ally in Asia' by a Pakistani military
leader, but this changed during the 1960s when
Pakistan went to war with India. During the
1980s the United States provided Pakistan with
military aid to support the anti-Soviet forces in
Afghanistan. In 1998, the United States
imposed economic sanctions on both Pakistan
and India after they carried out nuclear tests.

The relationship between Pakistan and the
United States improved once again after the
terrorist attacks in the United States in
September 2001. The terrorists were members
of al-Qaeda, a group based in Afghanistan and
led by Osama bin Laden. Following the attacks,
the president of the United States, George W.
Bush, announced a 'war on terrorism' and his
first action was to invade Afghanistan to
remove the Taliban regime and try to find
bin Laden. President Musharraf was put under
considerable international pressure to align his
government with the United States, despite
objections from within his own country.
Pakistan withdrew its diplomats from
Afghanistan, officially closed its borders and
arrested Islamic radicals. During the invasion of
Afghanistan, the United States airforce was
permitted to use Pakistani air space.

◀ The scene outside
the US consulate in
Karachi in March
2006, just after a car
bomb exploded. The
attack happened two
days before the visit
of the US president,
George W. Bush, to
Pakistan.

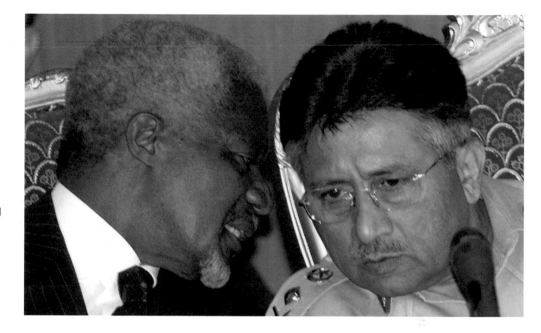

► President Pervez Musharraf listens to UN Secretary-General Kofi Annan during a Human Development Forum held in Islamabad, in 2002.

REGIONAL ORGANIZATIONS

Pakistan is a member of a number of regional organizations including The Organization of The Islamic Conference (OIC) and the South Asian Association for Regional Cooperation (SAARC). The OIC is an intergovernmental organization that is dedicated to representing the world's Muslims, and there is a permanent delegation from the OIC at the United Nations. SAARC is a South Asian organization whose members meet regularly to improve regional co-operation, to help economic development and to address social welfare problems of member states. Pakistan is also a member of the Commonwealth of Nations, an organization made up of the former territories of the British Empire. Pakistan left the Commonwealth in 1972 in protest at the Commonwealth's recognition of Bangladesh, but rejoined in 1989.

Focus on: Musharraf's balancing act

Musharraf's co-operation with the United States since 2001 has been met with hostility from Islamic fundamentalist groups within Pakistan and disapproval from other Muslim countries. Despite the fact that the United States has provided large sums of financial aid, President Musharraf nevertheless came under pressure from political parties within Pakistan to end the friendship with the United States. In 2002 there were violent riots and anti-US demonstrations in many Pakistani cities, and the US journalist Daniel Pearl was kidnapped and murdered by Islamic extremists in Pakistan. In 2003, President Musharraf himself survived two assassination attempts. As a result of these attacks Musharraf cracked down on the fundamentalists and directed the army to hunt for al-Qaeda and Taliban forces along the Pakistani border with Afghanistan. In 2004, President Bush designated Pakistan as a major non-NATO ally, a status that allows Pakistan to purchase advanced American military technology.

CHAPTER 9

Transport and Communications

Most of Pakistan's major road and rail routes run from north to south along the valley of the Indus River, with few routes into the mountains. Until 1990 little investment had been made in the transport network of the country.

ROADS

Much of the rural road network is in poor condition with roads consisting of a narrow strip of tarmac with dirt and gravel on either side. There are few roads through the mountains and they are frequently blocked by landslips or washed away by floods. During the 1990s, Pakistan started a huge project to construct a network of major roads to connect the main cities and towns. To help fund this expensive project, the government encouraged private companies to invest in the new roads. For example, the South Korean company, Daewoo, built the motorway between

Transport & communications data

- Total roads: 254,410 km/ 158,087 miles
- Total paved roads: 152,646 km/94,852 miles
- Total unpaved roads: 101,764 km/63,235 miles
- Total railways: 8,163 km/ 5,072 miles
- Major Airports: 91
- Cars per 1,000 people: 7
- Mobile phones per 1,000 people: 33
- Personal computers per 1,000 people: 5
- Internet users per 1,000 people: 13

Source: World Bank and CIA World Factbook

◀ In 2006, hundreds of auto rickshaw drivers took part in a rally in Karachi to protest about government plans to ban their vehicles because of the amount of pollution they produce.

Focus on: The Karakoram Highway

The Karakoram Highway was opened in 1982 after 20 years of construction. It connects Islamabad with Kashgar (also known as Kashi) in China, a distance of 1,300 km (808 miles) through the Karakoram mountains. Between 500 and 800 Pakistanis and a similar number of Chinese died during its construction. Not only is this road a vital trade link with China, it is also of military importance since it lies close to Kashmir.

▼ Tourists take a drive along the dramatic Karakoram Highway.

Islamabad and Lahore. It was completed in 1997 and until 2008, when the motorway will be handed over to the Pakistani government, Daewoo charges drivers a toll to use the road and is responsible for its maintenance.

CONGESTION

The number of vehicles on Pakistan's roads is increasing rapidly and the growth in traffic is causing major congestion problems, as many streets in Pakistan's cities were not designed for large numbers of vehicles. Emissions from cars and other vehicles are also partly responsible for high levels of air pollution in many cities (see page 54). In response to the traffic chaos in the city, the first mass transit project in Pakistan is being built in Karachi. This system is designed to move large numbers of people swiftly around the city. The mass transit system should be complete by 2008. Much of the first phase will be a light-rail link built over the existing road system. There are plans for a second phase to be built as soon as phase one is complete, which will involve an underground system.

RAILWAYS

The railway network is run by Pakistan Railways and it carries more than 65 million passengers each year. As well as passenger trains, there is an extensive freight transport system connecting the port of Karachi with the major cities and industrial centres. The rail network is being modernized, for example, the entire 1,760-kilometre (1,094-mile) track between Peshawar and Karachi has been replaced. New engines, passenger coaches and rail track have been purchased from China. The first of the new coaches started running on the Lahore to Karachi line in 2002 and it has been named the Karakoram Express.

PORTS

Karachi is the principal port of Pakistan. However, in 2002 construction started on a new port at Gwadar, near the Iranian border on the west coast of Baluchistan, to reduce the country's dependence on Karachi – which lies very close to the Indian border. The cost is huge, an estimated US$1.16 billion. The Chinese have provided much of the funding, construction engineers and technical expertise as the new port will provide China with vital access to major shipping routes and strengthen China's trade links with the Middle East and Europe. In addition, a new highway, also funded by the Chinese, is being built between Gwadar and Karachi.

COMMUNICATIONS

Television broadcasting started in 1964 and since then it has expanded to provide almost complete coverage of the country – even the mountainous regions. Satellite television arrived in the early 1990s, bringing international

▼ Railway stations in the major cities, such as this one in Karachi, are busy places.

◀ A woman walks past a wall of adverts for mobile phones in Karachi. Sales of mobile phones are booming in Pakistan, especially among young people.

broadcasting to nearly all homes. There are also cable television companies operating in the cities. The television channels were run by the state-owned Pakistan Television until 2002, when the government opened up the television market and allowed privately owned channels to broadcast, giving people more choice.

Until 2000 few people had a telephone. Landlines were found mostly in urban areas, and very few people in rural areas had access to a phone line. The arrival of the mobile phone in 1990 changed this. Since then, transmitters have been erected across the country, enabling people in both urban and rural areas to use a mobile phone. In 2004 the price of mobile phones and subscriptions came down and more people could afford them. By 2004 there were over 5 million mobile phones in use.

Internet use is also increasing. New high-speed fibre-optic connections link cities, allowing Pakistan to compete with other countries in fields such as information technology (IT). By 2006 it is predicted that more than 80 per cent of the population will have access to the Internet. However, the number of people actually logging on in Pakistan is still one of the lowest in the world, with an estimated 2 million Internet users in 2004.

? Did you know?

It is estimated that by 2007 the number of people in Pakistan owning a mobile phone will exceed the number owning a land-line telephone. The mobile phone in Pakistan has become a necessity rather than a luxury.

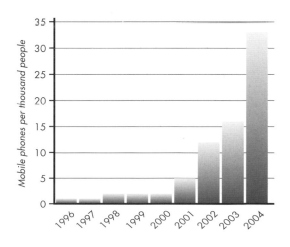

▲ Mobile phone use, 1996-2004

CHAPTER 10

Education and Health

Over the last 30 years the Pakistani government has spent increasing amounts of money on schools and health care. However, the population has been growing so fast that the services cannot keep up with demand.

SCHOOLING

Pakistan has one of the lowest literacy rates in the world. In 1998, the government launched a 12-year programme to eradicate illiteracy and provide all children with primary education. In 1998 only 40 per cent of adult Pakistanis could read and the aim was to double this by 2010. But by 2004 the adult literacy rate had increased to just 49.9 per cent.

Primary school education is free but not compulsory. Children attend primary school for five years. About 75 per cent of boys complete their primary education but only about 50 per cent of girls stay for all five years (see box on page 43). Class sizes can be as large as 50 or 60 children, and school facilities are often very basic, for example some schools lack toilets.

Children go to secondary school between the ages of 11 and 18. However, secondary education is not free so only about a quarter of children attend these schools. Pupils study four

◄ These Muslim students attend a *madrassa* in Lahore. Each day students spend many hours reading and learning about the Qu'ran.

Education and health

- Life expectancy at birth male: 64.1
- Life expectancy at birth female: 65.7
- Infant mortality rate per 1,000: 81
- Under five mortality rate per 1,000: 103
- Physicians per 1,000 people: 0.7
- Health expenditure as % of GDP: 2.4%
- Education expenditure as % of GDP: 2%
- Primary net enrolment: 56%
- Pupil-teacher ratio, primary: 46.9
- Adult literacy as % age 15+: 49.9%

Source: United Nations Agencies and World Bank

Focus on: Education for girls

Fewer than 50 per cent of girls go to school in Pakistan. Some parents feel it is a waste of time to educate girls, while others cannot afford the cost of secondary schools. Another reason for non-attendance is religion. Many Muslim girls are not allowed to leave home without an escort, so getting to school can be difficult, and there may be fears about young girls being seen by men outside the home. Often these problems can be overcome by simply building a wall around a school, so that girls can study in privacy. There has been a government programme over the last 20 years or so to persuade more parents to send their daughters to school and the literacy rate among women has risen from 21 per cent in 1980 to 34 per cent in 2004.

▲ A lesson at a school in Meerwala, in Punjab Province. In recent years the number of girls attending school in Pakistan has increased.

compulsory subjects, Urdu, English, Pakistani Studies and Islamic Studies, and choose four others. They sit the secondary school certificate at 15 years of age, which they have to pass if they want to attend higher secondary school until they are 18. At the end of higher secondary school, students take the higher secondary certificate which is required for university. Many children from richer families are sent to English-speaking schools, followed by university in Europe or North America.

RELIGIOUS SCHOOLS

There are as many as 40,000 private religious schools, called *madrassas*, in Pakistan. They educate between 1 and 3 million pupils, most of whom are boys between the ages of eight and 15. Many poor families send their boys to these schools as they offer free education. Most *madrassas* focus on teaching the Qu'ran, but the Pakistani government is trying to persuade these schools to teach a full range of subjects in return for funding.

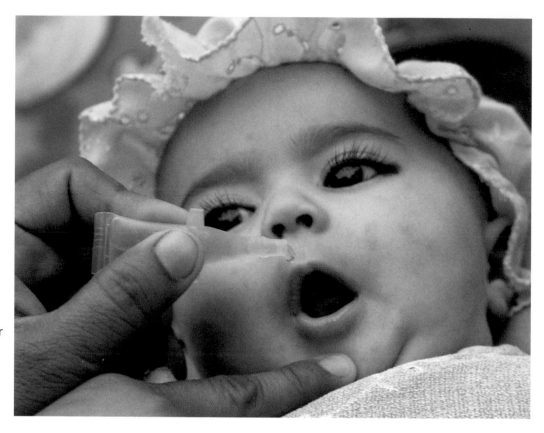

▶ The Pakistani government has a programme to vaccinate all children below the age of five for polio. The polio vaccine is given as drops in the mouth.

HEALTH

The health of the Pakistani people has improved over the last 30 years, but, as with education, health care is struggling to keep up with the growing number of people.

Each year, many children die from preventable diseases such as measles and diarrhoea. Over the last ten years there has been a massive vaccination programme and this is beginning to reduce the number of children dying from infectious diseases such as tetanus, polio and whooping cough. Although the number of children dying before they reach five years of age has decreased

(down from 130 deaths per 1,000 in 1990 to 103 deaths per 1,000 in 2003), their mortality rate is still higher than those of India (87 deaths per 1,000) and Bangladesh (69 deaths per 1,000).

WOMEN'S HEALTH

Women suffer from more health problems than men. Most of their health problems are linked to large family sizes and the frequency of giving birth. The average family size is five to six children, much higher than elsewhere in South Asia – for example in India the average number is three children. Every year in Pakistan there are about five million births and as many as 30,000 women die of pregnancy-related complications. The underlying problems that affect women's health include poverty, illiteracy, women's low status in society, inadequate water supplies and poor sanitation. One way to reduce

? Did you know?

Each year about 270,000 people in Pakistan catch tuberculosis, a disease of the lungs caused by a bacterium. It can be treated with antibiotics.

this death rate is through family planning and the use of contraceptives. However, contraceptives need to be used correctly if they are to stop pregnancy. Now that more women can read, they can follow the instructions on the packs and successfully prevent pregnancy.

One government project to help improve women's health is called the Lady Health Worker Programme. Many women have problems leaving the house because they need permission from their husbands, and they cannot have male visitors. The Lady Health Worker Programme provides female health workers to visit women in their homes. Their job is to make sure that women are familiar with all issues associated with their health, teaching some basic health care and providing family planning. In 2005, about 43,000 women were serving as Lady Health Workers in their home villages.

POLLUTION AND HEALTH

Many health problems are caused by air and water pollution. Raw sewage is dumped into rivers and the presence of harmful bacteria in the water causes water-borne diseases such as dysentery and cholera. Cars are the main source of air pollution, mostly caused by poorly maintained engines and the burning of poor-quality fuel (see page 54). Up to 6.5 million people are hospitalized each year for illnesses related to air pollution.

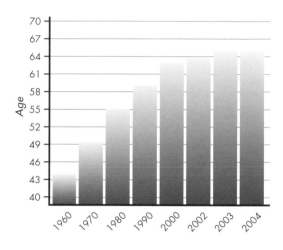

▲ Life expectancy at birth 1960-2004

▼ The Shaukat Khanum Memorial Hospital in Lahore is a world-class cancer hospital. About 2,500 new patients are treated each year.

CHAPTER 11

Culture and Religion

Pakistani society is multilingual and multicultural. Traditional Islamic family values are highly respected. Over the last few decades a middle class has emerged in many of the larger cities for whom education, home ownership and career prospects are important. In contrast, the people of northwest Pakistan are highly conservative and practise centuries-old customs.

FOOD

Pakistani food is a mix of Middle Eastern and northern Indian traditions. Typically, chicken, lamb, mutton (sheep), beef or prawns are cooked in hot and spicy curry sauces. These are accompanied by rice, vegetables and flat breads such as *nan* and *chapatis*. A main course is followed by milky desserts, such as bread cooked in milk and sugar, or rice and milk. Sometimes a meal is finished with *paan*, which is a mixture of tobacco paste, spices and betel nut spread on a betel leaf. The main drinks are spiced milky tea (known as *chai*), sugar cane juice and *lassi* (a yoghurt drink).

Celebratory dishes are served on festival days. For example, a special dessert of vermicelli cooked in milk with almonds and pistachios is served on Eid ul-Fitr, while the traditional dish at a wedding ceremony is chicken curry and rice.

? *Did you know?*

Sharbat is a fruit drink, squeezed from fruits such as pomegranates, apples, melons and mangoes. It is a Mughal drink and was the inspiration for modern-day 'sherbets'.

▼ This shopkeeper in Rawalpindi is frying sweetened breads on a large iron griddle.

MUSIC

The most popular music of Pakistan is *Qawwali*, which dates back to the 13th century. Typically, *Qawwali* consists of a lead vocalist, two back-up vocalists and a number of percussionists. The rhythm is traditionally played on a type of hand drum called a *dholak*. Poetic verses are usually mixed with a chorus and instrumental passages. Recently, some musicians have mixed *Qawwali* music with Western pop music and this has become popular with many young people. Among the best-known musicians are Nusrat Fateh Ali Khan, the Sabri Brothers and the Rizwan-Muazzam Qawwali Group.

▲ Pakistani brides at a ceremony in 2005. One woman wears a *burqa* which completely covers her body, with just a slit for her eyes.

NATIONAL DRESS

The national dress is the *shalwar-kameez*, the combination of a long shirt over loose baggy trousers. Woman wear their *shalwar-kameez* in a variety of colours and designs, whereas men tend to stick to plain black or white. Muslim women are expected to wear conservative clothing such as the *shalwar-kameez* together with a veil or sometimes a *burqa*, which is a head-to-toe covering over the *shalwar-kameez*. Pathan men also wear sleeveless embroidered vests (waistcoats) over their *shalwar-kameez*. The Afghan Pathans wear turbans while the Pakistani Pathans generally wear caps of various shapes.

Focus on: Western influences

Increasing globalization has strengthened the influence of Western culture in Pakistan, especially among the rich and the better-educated who have easy access to Western goods, television and food. Western-style clothing is commonly worn by the upper classes, and many Western food chains, such as McDonalds, have opened outlets in Pakistan. At the same time, there is also a reactionary movement within Pakistan that wants to turn away from all Western influences and return to a more traditional Islamic way of life, with an emphasis on religion.

Focus on: Lollywood

Pakistan's film industry is often referred to as 'Lollywood' because it is based in Lahore. The films all tend to be very similar, with love songs, dancing and fistfights, and good always defeating evil. During the 1960s, more than 200 films were made each year and the stars of these movies were hugely popular in Pakistan. Then the film industry went into a decline due to lack of investment, and during the 1990s barely 40 films were made a year. There was a revival in 2002 when Javed Sheikh, a well-known director, invested in digital equipment to make his hit movie *Yeh Dil Aap Ka Huwa (This Heart Belongs to You)*. Since 2002 a number of major digital films have been made and the future of Lollywood is now looking brighter.

◀ Huge posters advertise the latest films being shown in Karachi cinemas.

RELIGION

About 96 per cent of Pakistanis are Muslims, the majority being Sunni Muslims while the others are Shi'a Muslims. The remaining 4 per cent of the population is made up of Christian, Hindu and other faiths. These minorities are given fewer rights than Muslim citizens, for example non-Muslims may only vote for non-Muslim candidates at elections. There has been considerable violence between the different religious groups over the years, in particular between Sunni and Shi'a Muslims.

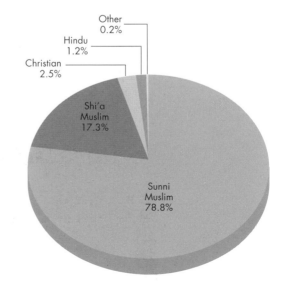

Other
0.2%

Hindu
1.2%

Christian
2.5%

Shi'a
Muslim
17.3%

Sunni
Muslim
78.8%

▶ Pakistan's major religions

FESTIVALS

Pakistanis celebrate a number of Muslim festivals, the most important being Eid ul-Fitr, Eid ul-Adha, and Eid Milad-un-Nabi. During these festivals Pakistani people wear their best clothes to attend special prayers.

Eid ul-Fitr (or simply Eid) marks the end of the month of fasting known as Ramadan. In Pakistan, the night before Eid is called Chand Raat, or 'night of the moon' and young women paint each other's hands with henna and wear colourful bangles. On the day of Eid, families attend prayers, then visit friends and relatives to eat a celebration meal and exchange gifts. It is a day of forgiveness, peace, fellowship and unity.

Eid ul Adha celebrates Abraham's willingness to sacrifice his son to Allah. During the festival, Muslims sacrifice domestic animals, such as a sheep or goat, and share the meat amongst their neighbours, relatives, and with the poor. The festival of Eid Milad-un-Nabi celebrates the Prophet Muhammad's birthday.

There are a number of public holidays too, including Pakistan Day on 23 March (the anniversary of the demand by the All India Muslim League in Lahore in 1940 for a separate independent state for Muslims) and Independence Day on 14 August.

Focus on: Honour killings

Each year hundreds of Pakistani women die in so-called 'honour killings'. These are women who are considered to have brought shame on their family. There are many reasons given for killing in the name of honour, including illicit sexual relationships, rape, marriage without consent and seeking divorce. Women are usually killed by members of their own family, often despite the fact that their alleged 'crime' may be unproven. Although honour killings are crimes in Pakistani law, the law is almost never enforced, and the murderers in such killings are rarely prosecuted.

◀ A man sells paper toys to celebrate the Muslim festival of Eid Milad-un-Nabi in Karachi.

CHAPTER 12

Leisure and Tourism

The warm weather of southern Pakistan enables people to live an outdoor life. A favourite activity for young people living near the coast is to go to the beach. But it is very different in the mountains, where people tend to stay indoors during the long, cold winters and only participate in sports during the short summer months.

SPORTS

Pakistan is a nation that loves sport and Pakistani men participate in many sports, especially cricket, hockey, squash and tennis. Each year, a National Games is held covering a range of track and field events together with basketball, volleyball, cycling, weightlifting and wrestling. Pakistani teams also take part in the Olympics, Asian Games, Islamic Games and Commonwealth Games.

The Pakistani people are passionate about cricket. It is the national sport and most young boys play cricket. The national cricket team is revered and their successes and failures on the field are reported in the newspapers and on radio and television. There is great rivalry between the Pakistani and Indian teams. In 1992 Pakistan won the Cricket World Cup under the captaincy of Imran Khan.

The men's Pakistani field hockey team is one of the best in the world. The team has won gold

◀ Hockey matches between Pakistan (in dark green) and India (in blue) are fiercely contested. This match took place in India in 2004, and Pakistan won 2-1.

◄ Polo is a fast-moving game played on horseback. This match is being played in the magnificent setting of the Shandur Pass in the Hindu Kush mountains.

medals at all the major hockey events, including the Olympics, World Cup, Asian Games and Asian Cup. At the Athens Olympics in 2004, Pakistan did not win a medal but their star player, Sohail Abbas, was the highest scoring player with 11 goals.

Polo is incredibly popular in the mountainous regions. This is a sport in which two opposing teams of horsemen use a stick to move a ball around a pitch and score goals. Polo dates back to the 6th century BC when it was a training game for the cavalry. The game is played by two teams of six players who play for two

25-minute periods with a ten-minute break. The annual polo tournament played between teams from Chitral and Gilgit is fast becoming a major event on the tourist calendar.

A popular sport in South Asia is *kabbadi*. In this sport, there are two teams of seven players. The teams take it in turns to send a raider into the opposing team's half of the pitch, tag members of that team, and then return home. Any player who is tagged leaves the field. The raid must take place without the raider taking a breath, so to prove this, the raider constantly chants. In Pakistan the player chants 'kabbadi'.

Focus on: Women and sport

In general, sport in Pakistan is for men while the girls concentrate on indoor activities such as needlework and cookery. However, some young women participate in sport, despite the barriers. Most women in Pakistan do not play sport in public places in case they are observed by men. Instead they play on private playing fields and with only women spectators. They also wear baggy trousers and long-sleeved shirts to cover their legs and arms completely. A few women have competed in other Muslim countries. For example, Pakistani women won a gold medal for golf at the 2005 Women's Islamic Games in Tehran, Iran.

► The Kalasha people live in three valleys near Chitral in the Hindu Kush. The women wear black gowns with elaborate and colourful decorations.

TOURISM

For a long time tourism in Pakistan has been under-developed, largely a result of the political unrest and wars in the region. Most visitors to the country are Pakistan-born people returning to see their families. However, the number of foreign tourists is increasing, especially in the mountainous regions where trekking and mountaineering are growing in popularity.

The northern areas of Pakistan are very scenic and there are many old army fortresses, towers and other architecturally interesting buildings with a long history. Some of the most beautiful valleys are found in the Chitral and Hunza Mountains in the Hindu Kush. Three isolated valleys near Chitral are famous for being the home of a small ethnic group known as the Kalasha people, who claim they are descended from soldiers in the army of Alexander the Great.

The Murree Hills and the Gallies are located about 55 km (34 miles) from Islamabad, at an altitude of 2,286 m (7,500 ft). They are the most popular summer resorts in Pakistan for wealthy Pakistanis and foreign tourists, as they experience warm weather in contrast to the oppressively hot and humid weather on the plains. The resorts are equipped with modern facilities including resort hotels, golf courses, chairlifts and cable cars.

HISTORIC SITES

Punjab Province has a particularly rich history, and Lahore is usually regarded as Pakistan's cultural capital, attracting a large number of the country's tourists. The city was conquered by

Tourism in Pakistan

- Tourist arrivals, millions: 0.648
- Earnings from tourism in US$: 763,000,000
- Tourism as % foreign earnings: 4.7%
- Tourist departures, millions: n/a
- Expenditure on tourism in US$: 1,590,000,000

Source: World Bank

the Mughals and all of its important monuments were built by them, for example the Royal Fort, the Badshahi Mosque (see page 10), Wazir Khan's Mosque and the Tombs of Jehangir. In the south of Punjab Province, around Multan and Bahawalpur, there are many Muslim shrines, mosques and forts, featuring the towers, domes and courtyards, and bright colours and geometric shapes of much Islamic architecture. Amongst the most

important buildings are the forts at Bahawalpur and Multan, the shrines of Sheikh Bahauddin Zakaria and Hazrat Shams Tabrizi at Multan and the Tomb of Bib Jiwandi near Bahawalpur.

The ruins of ancient settlements dating back thousands of years have been excavated in the Indus Valley. They include the settlements of Moenjodaro and Harappa (see page 8).

Focus on: K2

K2, the second highest mountain in the world, is so named because it is the second peak of the Karakoram range. It was first conquered in 1954 by two Italians, Lino Lacedelli and Achille Compagnoni. Since that time about 200 teams have successfully climbed the mountain. However, it is a technically difficult mountain to climb – much harder than Everest – and there have been 50 deaths on the mountain, mostly on the descent.

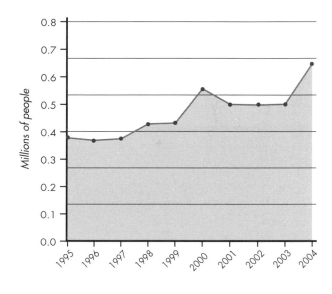

▲ Changes in international tourism, 1995-2004

◄ The tomb (mausoleum) of the fourth Mughal emperor, Jehangir (1569-1627), lies about 5 km (3 miles) outside Lahore. It is built from red sandstone and marble.

CHAPTER 13

Environment and Conservation

Pakistan suffers from a range of environmental problems, most of which originate from the rapid increase in population, economic expansion and the exploitation of resources. In recent years the government of Pakistan has focused on producing more food, meeting the population's growing energy needs and on increasing economic growth. Controlling environmental pollution has not been a high priority. However the effects of air pollution from traffic fumes and industrial emissions, and water pollution from industrial wastes and sewage, are harming the health of the people.

AIR POLLUTION

In Karachi and Lahore the level of air pollution is estimated to be 20 times higher than World Health Organization standards and it is still rising. Islamabad is almost always shrouded in a thick layer of smog that hides the views of the surrounding hills. The major causes of air pollution are coal-fired power stations, industrial emissions and traffic. The coal is of poor quality and when it is burned to generate electricity it releases sulphur dioxide, a major cause of acid rain. Acid rain (caused by water being more acidic than normal) harms the health of trees, lakes and rivers as well as damaging buildings. The areas of the country most affected are Karachi and the central Punjab.

Traffic fumes are another cause of air pollution. The average Pakistani vehicle emits as much as 25 times more carbon dioxide and 3.5 times more acid rain-forming chemicals than the average vehicle in the United States. There are regulations to control vehicle emissions but they are not strictly enforced. The main cause is the use of poor-quality fuel that is high in lead and sulphur. Although unleaded petrol is available,

▶ Although the burning of rubber has been banned, many factories in Pakistan, such as this brick kiln in Peshawar, continue to use rubber as a fuel, producing a thick, black polluting smoke.

most vehicles still run on leaded fuels and few vehicles are fitted with catalytic converters. Motorized rickshaws are a particular problem in cities as they use poor-quality fuels. The Canadian International Development Agency is working in some cities in Pakistan to convert rickshaws so they can run on LPG (liquefied petroleum gas), which is much cleaner.

DESERTIFICATION

Desertification is a problem in the arid regions of the country, especially in Baluchistan. This is caused by overgrazing of arid land by herds of sheep and goats. Once the vegetation cover is lost, the soil is exposed and at risk of wind erosion. An estimated 5 million hectares (12 million acres) are believed to be at risk from such erosion. The problems can be overcome by replanting and by improved management of the grazing herds.

SALINIZATION

Poor water management in the irrigated areas of Punjab and Sindh provinces is causing major environmental problems. Often, too much water is emptied on to the fields where it causes waterlogging. In the high temperatures, water evaporates from the surface, leaving salts behind. This build-up of salt in the soil is called salinization. Soil that is damaged by salinization is too salty to grow most types of crops. In 1998, more than 6 million hectares (14.8 million acres) in Pakistan were thought to be saline and unable to support crops.

The problem can be overcome with better irrigation management and by growing varieties of crops that are more tolerant of high salt levels. In some cases, it is possible to wash out the salts by flooding the fields, although this uses a lot of valuable water.

▲ This farmer in Shimshal is altering the path of an irrigation channel. If irrigation is not carried out correctly the soil can be damaged by waterlogging.

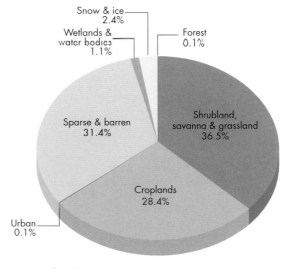

Snow & ice 2.4%
Wetlands & water bodies 1.1%
Forest 0.1%
Shrubland, savanna & grassland 36.5%
Sparse & barren 31.4%
Croplands 28.4%
Urban 0.1%

▲ Types of habitat

▲ Children in Karachi wash in filthy water. Every year in Pakistan, hundreds of thousands of children die from water-borne diseases.

WATER POLLUTION

A safe source of drinking water is essential for health, but millions of people in Pakistan do not have access to safe water. All sorts of pollutants are emptied into rivers, lakes and the sea. They include untreated sewage, chemical wastes from factories, and pesticides and fertilizers from agriculture. Many industrial sites have been built with little planning and with no waste water treatment plants, so all forms of toxic chemicals end up in the water supply. As a consequence, an estimated 40 per cent of deaths are related to water-borne diseases. There is much that could be done to combat water pollution, but most important is to identify those industries that produce the most pollution and strictly enforce the National Environmental Quality Standards. This would require these industries to treat their waste water to make it safe.

DEFORESTATION

Wood has long been an important energy source in Pakistan's rural areas. However the rapid expansion of the population has led to an increased demand for firewood as well as for timber for building. There has been extensive deforestation, both of mangrove swamps along the coast and of forested slopes in the Himalayas. The deforestation in the mountains has led to soil erosion on a large scale. The forested slopes protect the thin mountain soils and the roots of the trees bind the soil. When the trees are felled and the protection removed, the water can flow straight off the slopes, carrying the soil with it. This can cause landslides and flooding.

In 1993, the government prepared a Master Plan for Forestry Development which aimed to increase the forested area by 10 per cent by 2018. Commercial plantations of fast-growing plants such as eucalyptus and bamboo have been planted in irrigated areas, and there has been some reforestation in the mountains. However, there is a very small budget and this restricts the amount of replanting and conservation that can be carried out.

NATIONAL PARKS

National parks in Pakistan were established in the 1970s to protect the country's forests and wildlife. The first national park was Lal Suhanra (near Bahawalpur in Punjab Province) in 1972, followed in 1974 by Kirthar National Park in southern Sindh, which was set up to protect the ibex, Chinkara gazelle and Urial sheep. The Khunjerab National Park in the Hunza Mountains followed in 1975. It is one of the country's most important regions for alpine biodiversity, and at 5,000 m (16,404 ft) it is also one of the highest parks in the world. It protects the habitat of endangered species such as the Marco Polo sheep, blue sheep, snow leopard and snow cock (a type of bird). There are now 15 national parks in Pakistan covering 714,000 hectares (1,764,000 acres). There are also many wildlife sanctuaries and game reserves, one biosphere reserve (a protected area of high biodiversity) and two wetland sites (areas of importance for wildfowl such as swans and ducks).

Focus on: Oil exploration vs wildlife

In 1997 great controversy erupted when the government decided to allow oil and gas exploration in Kirthar National Park, which lies just to the north of Karachi. The park was established to protect rare and threatened species. Conservation groups, both within and outside Pakistan, tried to challenge the decision as it violated Pakistan's international commitment to protect biodiversity. But the government simply changed the environmental laws, allowing the exploration to take place. The oil companies claim that any development following the discovery of oil and gas in the park would have minimal impact on the environment, and provide local jobs.

Environmental and conservation data

- Forested area as % total land area: 0.1%
- Protected area as % total land area: 9.2%
- Number of protected areas: 205

SPECIES DIVERSITY

Category	Known species	Threatened species
Mammals	188	19
Breeding birds	237	17
Reptiles	189	9
Amphibians	17	n/a
Fish	137	3
Plants	4,950	2

Source: World Resources Institute

► The Khunjerab National Park lies high in the mountains of northern Pakistan. It was established to protect alpine species of plants and animals.

CHAPTER 14

Future Challenges

Pakistan is going to have to tackle a number of issues in the future, including its expanding population, environmental damage, the status of women and the problem of Kashmir. There are also issues associated with economic growth and the threat from terrorism.

THE ROLE OF WOMEN

Although the status of women in Pakistan has improved in recent years, there is still much to be done. Several groups such as the Women's Action Forum are tackling issues such as a woman's legal status as well as everyday matters such as the dress code. Improved status for women may help to reduce the rate at which the population increases, as educated women have a better understanding of health issues.

ECONOMIC FUTURE

There are a number of problems facing the stability of the Pakistani economy including the level of foreign debt and a rising inflation rate. The foreign debt is a great burden on the country and has a direct impact on the amounts available for social services such as education and health. The government is tackling this problem by tightening up financial controls in government departments so that less is wasted. In 2006, President Bush visited Pakistan and promised to try to secure a US$3 billion aid package over five years. If successful, this would provide support to the military in the struggle against terrorism and provide more resources for education and health.

KASHMIR – THE FUTURE

In January 2004, Pakistan and India started peace talks. India would like to formalize the current boundary between the two parts of Kashmir and make it an international border, an idea supported by the United States and the UK. Pakistan objects as it claims that this does not take into account the wishes of the Muslim population in Indian-controlled Kashmir. Pakistan's preferred outcome is that the whole of Kashmir becomes part of Pakistan. However, although the majority of the population on the Indian side is Muslim there are also substantial numbers of Hindus and Buddhists who would object to joining Pakistan. An alternative is for the whole of Kashmir to become an

◄ In April 2005 an important step in the peace process took place when the first bus crossed from Pakistan-controlled to India-controlled Kashmir.

◀ President Bush and President Musharraf respond to a question during a joint press conference in March 2006. President Bush visited Pakistan to strengthen the relationship between the United States and Pakistan.

independent state, but this option is favoured by neither Pakistan nor India, as both would have to give up territory, and both countries fear that such a move would encourage other groups seeking independence. So currently the situation is one of stalemate, with neither side wanting to give way.

PAKISTAN AND TERRORISM

Pakistan has given support to the global fight against terrorists and President Musharraf has clamped down on groups directly linked with al-Qaeda, even though these actions have not been popular with some of the radical Islamic groups in the country. However, Pakistan has continued to allow militant Kashmiris to operate in the country. The Pakistani government sees these militants as allies in its conflict with India, while the Indian government sees them as terrorists. In July 2006, seven bombs exploded on packed commuter trains in Mumbai (Bombay) in India, killing more than 160 people and injuring hundreds. The Indian government blamed the militant Kashmiri groups, and stated that the peace talks could not continue until the Pakistani government cracked down on these terrorists. Pakistan needs to be seen to be fighting all terrorist groups, whatever their cause, if it is to win international support.

A BALANCING ACT

Pakistan has a difficult balancing act to perform over the next few years. The many ethnic groups within Pakistan have different demands, some wanting more recognition while others want independence. Meanwhile, China and the United States are underpinning the Pakistani economy with financial support, but in return both want more influence in the running of the country.

During 2005 the political situation in Afghanistan had become more stable and there was a great increase in trade between the two countries. However, during 2006 the situation in Afghanistan changed for the worse. The Afghanistani president, Hamid Karzai, claimed that Pakistan was not doing enough to arrest members of al-Qaeda sheltering in Pakistan. The relationship between the two countries deteriorated and President Bush called the leaders to Washington for talks. The relationship between the two countries remains tense. However, Pakistan's relationship with India is improving. The economy of India is booming and if the Pakistani government decides to cooperate more with India it could share the benefits of its growing markets. The future for the country could be very prosperous.

Timeline

c. 4000 BC Indus Valley site of early civilization.

c. 1700 BC Aryans from Central Asia move into region.

327 BC Alexander the Great invades from the north and defeats army of King Porus.

322 BC Chandragupta Maurya founds the Mauryan Empire.

272-232 BC Reign of Ashoka who spreads Buddhism in the region.

195 BC King Demetrius of Bactria invades.

75 BC Scythians invade.

50 BC Parthians invade.

AD 120 Kushan dynasty established.

712 Imad-ud-din Muhammad bin Qasim, an Arab from the Middle East, invades Sindh.

997-1030 Reign of Mahmud Ghaznavi and creation of Ghaznavid Empire.

1187 Muhammad of Ghor brings Ghaznavid Empire to an end.

1206-1526 Delhi Sultanate.

1526 Region becomes part of the Mughal Empire.

1615 British East India Company establishes base in India.

1707 End of Mughal dominance.

1857 War of Independence between British and Indians.

1858 Punjab and Sindh along with India become part of the British Empire.

1907 All-India Muslim League established.

1940 All India Muslim League demands a completely independent state of Indian Muslims.

1947 Partition of India – millions die in subsequent unrest. Pakistan becomes an independent country made up of East and West Pakistan. First Kashmir War with India.

1954 First ascent of K2.

1956 Pakistan becomes the Islamic Republic of Pakistan with a new constitution.

1958 Military take over and establish Martial Law.

1968 General Ayub Khan declares martial law.

1962 New constitution.

1965 Second Kashmir War with India.

1967 Islamabad becomes capital city of Pakistan.

1969 Martial law declared again.

1970 Awami League based in East Pakistan wins a majority in the Pakistani government, causing unrest across Pakistan.

1971 East Pakistan declares independence and forms the new state of Bangladesh. War with India and subsequent defeat. Zulfiqar Ali Bhutto elected as president.

1972 Establishment of first national park.

1973 New constitution published.

1977 Zulfiqar Ali Bhutto overthrown in military coup. General Zia-ul-Haq imposes martial law and starts a programme of Islamization.

1980s Millions of Afghan refugees flee to Pakistan.

1988 General Zia-ul-Haq dies in a plane crash and Benazir Bhutto becomes the first woman to govern an Islamic country.

1990 Benazir Bhutto loses election and Nawaz Sharif is elected prime minister.

1992 Pakistan wins Cricket World Cup.

1993 Benazir Bhutto wins election and is prime minister again.

1996 Benazir Bhutto's government dismissed on charge of corruption.

1997 Nawaz Sharif becomes prime minister.

1998 Pakistan becomes a declared nuclear power when it conducts nuclear bomb tests.

1999 Kargil Conflict in Kashmir. General Pervez Musharraf leads a military coup. Nawaz Sharif found guilty of corruption and exiled to Saudi Arabia.

2001 Pakistan cuts contact with the Taliban in Afghanistan and joins United States and its 'war on terrorism'.

2003 President Musharraf survives an assassination attempt.

2004 Shaukat Aziz becomes prime minister. Pakistan and India agree to a ceasefire in Kashmir.

2005 Cross-border bus services resume in Kashmir. Powerful earthquake kills 86,000 people and injures hundreds of thousands in northern Pakistan and Kashmir.

2006 President Bush visits Pakistan and promises to secure a US$3 billion aid package over five years.

Glossary

Acid rain Rain that is more acidic than normal, caused by acids, such as sulphur dioxide, dissolving in water.

Buddhism A world religion that started about 2,500 years ago. The founder of Buddhism was Siddhartha Gautama (c.563-c.483 BC), who became known as the Buddha – the 'enlightened one'.

Catalytic converter A device that allows vehicles to run on unleaded fuel.

Constituency A voting district in which people elect a representative.

Constitution An agreed set of rules and laws.

Corruption Dishonest behaviour, for example by a government official.

Coup A sudden change of government by illegal means, often by military force.

Deforestation Clearance of forest by cutting and burning to put the land to another use.

Delta The mouth of a river where the river spilts into many small tributaries.

Democracy A political system in which representatives are chosen by the people in free elections.

Desertification The process by which fertile land becomes desert through the action of people.

Erosion The wearing away of land or soil by the action of wind, water, or ice.

Ethnic Describes a way of grouping people according to shared customs, beliefs and often language.

Federation Relating to a country that is made up of a number of self-governing states or regions.

Foreign debt The amount a country owes to overseas governments and organizations.

Foreign exchange Where money or currency from one country is exchanged for that of another.

Fundamentalists People who have very traditional beliefs, often about their religion.

Gross Domestic Product (GDP) The total value of goods and services produced by a country.

Henna A type of dye from the henna plant that is often used to colour skin or hair temporarily.

Hinduism A native religion of India. Hindus worship many gods and goddesses and believe that a person is reborn many times into many different lives.

Hydroelectric power (HEP) Electricity generated by harnessing the power of moving water.

Inflation The measurement of how much the price of a selection of goods which are necessary for life in a particular country changes in one year.

Infrastructure All the public facilities and services needed by a country to function, including roads, schools, hospitals, sewerage and water systems.

Irrigation The artificial watering of crops.

Islam A major world religion based on a belief in one God (Allah) and the teachings of his prophet, Muhammad.

Islamization Describes a movement that puts strong emphasis on Islamic values and traditions.

Liquefied Petroleum Gas (LPG) A fuel made from a mixture of butane and propane and stored as a liquid.

Martial law The laws put in place when the military take power, when civil laws are suspended.

Mass transit system A public transport system designed to move large numbers of people.

Monsoon The seasonal winds that are generated by the difference in air temperatures over the Asian landmass and the sea, which bring regular rainfall to the Indian subcontinent.

Mosque A Muslim place of worship.

Nomadic A way of life in which people move from place to place.

Partition The term given to the division of India into separate parts at independence.

Plateau High ground with a flat top.

Qu'ran The holy book of Islam.

Rickshaw A small, two-wheeled cart for one passenger and pulled by one person.

Salinization The accumulation of salts in the top layer of soil.

Sanctions A ban, usually on trading, also known as a boycott.

Sharia Islamic law based on the Qu'ran.

Shi'a Describes Muslims who believe that religious authority can lie only with direct descendants of the Prophet Muhammad.

Silt Fine particles of soil in rivers, ponds or lakes.

Socialist A person who supports socialism, which favours the public ownership of major industries and distribution of wealth.

Sunni The largest branch of Islam, it describes those Muslims who believe that religious authority lies with the person best able to uphold the customs and traditions (the *sunnah*) of Islam.

Taliban A group of fundamentalist Muslims who seized power in Afghanistan in 1996.

Temperate Describes a climate that is neither too hot nor too cold, with definite seasons.

Terrorist A person who uses violence to achieve their political aims.

Toxic Poisonous, harmful.

Further Information

BOOKS TO READ

Notes from My Travels: Visits with Refugees in Africa, Cambodia, Pakistan and Ecuador
Angelina Jolie
(Simon and Schuster, 2003)

Himalaya
Michael Palin
(Weidenfeld & Nicolson Illustrated, 2004)

Religion in Focus: Islam in Today's World
Deborah Weston, Janet Orchard, Sally Lynch, Claire Clinton
(Hodder Murray, 2005)

Troubled World: Conflict, India and Pakistan
David Downing
(Heinemann Library, 2003)

The Growth and Influence of Islam in the Nations of Asia and Central Asia: Pakistan
Clarissa Aykroyd
(Mason Crest Publishers, 2005)

Country Files: Pakistan
Ian Graham
(Franklin Watts, 2005)

USEFUL WEBSITES

http://www.pak.gov.pk/
Official website giving information on the government, industry, culture and visiting the country.

http://www.wwfpak.org/
Work of the WWF in Pakistan.

There are a number of websites that are devoted to the aid work that has taken place since the earthquake in October 2005. They include:
http://www.directrelief.org/sections/our_work/southasia_earthquake.html

http://www.ri.org/countries.php?cid=16
Relief International

http://www.savethechildren.org.uk
Save the Children

http://www.unicef.org/infobycountry/pakistan.html
Update on UNICEF projects in Pakistan, especially aid work following the earthquake.

Index

Page numbers in **bold** indicate pictures.

About the Author

Sally Morgan is an experienced author of children's books and has written on a wide range of topics including nature and conservation, science, geography and environmental issues.

She is particularly interested in wildlife and conservation and travels extensively to watch and photograph plants and animals.